Brown Sugar

Azúcar Morena

Maribel Sandoval

ISBN: 9781790192380

DEDICATION

In loving memory of my two brothers and boyfriend.
Fernando Sandoval and Steve Sandoval I and my
Dominicano; Junior Cedeño Sanchez.
To my strong beautiful mother Antonia Gutierrez, for
showing me how to love unconditionally. Lastly, my father
Jose Sandoval, the first man I ever loved.

CONTENTS

Maribel Sandoval

1 NOTE TO SELF/NOTA PERSONAL

Como dice mi mamá... estoy como Santa Elena, entre mas vieja más buena.

Miss Universe

I am no Miss Universe
I do not have the fattest ass or the smallest waist
Or the prettiest symmetrical face
But I can walk into a room and have everyone look up at
me
And wonder... Who is she?

Miss Universo

No soy ningún Miss Universo
No tengo el mejor cuerpo, o la cintura mas chiquita
O la cara mas bonita
Pero puedo entrar a un cuarto y todos se voltean a ver
Quien es ella?... Todos quieren saber

Beauty is her name

Growing up she always saw beauty in everything but herself

She didn't think she was pretty, because she didn't look like everyone else

Blonde hair, blue eyes, fare skin, always seemed to be in

She didn't have any of that, so she never fit in

She asked her mother one day, " Why am I not pretty?"

Her mother said "You're not; you're beautiful like your name."

It was that day that she discovered that beauty is her name

Latin meaning for Maribel: Beautiful Marie

Se llama bella

Cuando era niña, pensaba que era fea
Porque solo los de ojos azules y piel clara, eran bonitos
Si tenías pelo oscuro y piel morena, eras feito
Hasta que un día le pregunte a mi mama, "Mama, ¿porque no estoy bonita?"
Y mi mama respondió, "No eres bonita, eres bella, que no ves que en tu nombre ya tienes la palabra dentro de ella"

Maribel: Bella Mari

Not my looks

It is my mind that will raise your child, not my looks
So I ask that you love me for my soul
For it is my heart that will keep our family whole

El corazón no tiene cara

Mi belleza no va criar a tus hijos
Por eso te pido que te enamores de mi alma
Porque es mi alma y corazón que los va cuidar
Ya cuando estén grandes mi belleza ya no va estar

Move different

Sometimes in life, you have to move different if you want something different
One day you might get tired of the same old, and you're going to want something different
One day what bothered you will have you feeling indifferent
Stop accepting what you've been used to
It's ok to change the song to something you don't usually move to

Muévete diferente

En la vida, tienes que moverte diferente si quieres algo
diferente
Algún día te cansaras de lo mismo de ayer, y te vas a
querer mover
En vez de una balada, échate una cumbia
Para que veas que no hay montaña que no se derrumba

I can do bad all by myself

I rather be single, than settle for an uncommitted soul
I'm pretty sure I deserve more
Better yet, I know
But if that is all you have for me, then get out of my face
I can do bad all by myself, I didn't need you anyway

Puedo ser feliz solita

Prefiero estar soltera que con un alma que no puede
comprometerse a nada
Para que quiero un estorbo o un bueno para nada
Yo puedo ser feliz solita
Mejor sola, quien con alguien que solo chinga y me grita

Miss you

You've ever missed you?
That glow, when your guard was down
When you smiled all the time instead of frowned
I get it, the past hasn't been the best
But God chose you, and nonetheless
You punish yourself over and over
Don't you see, there is a reason why he chose you over her?
I get that your soul hurts
But a brighter day will begin when you forgive yourself
Live your life, take chances and forget everyone else
Be selfish
Stop trying to save the helpless
Give your power to others less
Let them drown in their own mess
And bring her back out
Promise yourself to never be without – You

Me extraño

Que no te extrañas?
A quien engañas
Si tu misma sabes que has cambiado
Ya no eres la misma del pasado
Antes eras mas sonriente
Y te valía lo que decía la gente
Porque no dejas de estar al pendiente
Deja de cuidar a todos los que no se cuidan
Rezales un Ave María
Y que se vayan mucho a la jodida
Que tu te necesitas a ti más que ellos
Así es que se vayan con sus problemas, pero lejos… muy
lejos
Y deja de extrañarte
Y veras que bonito es todo cuando vez con otros lentes

Times like these

She used to pray for times like these
To be alone and at ease
To no longer waste her make up for her mind is already
made up
And her thoughts clear when she wakes up
She had made the choice to stay away from those
that preach more than they practice
You know, the kind that have loyalty backwards
She no longer bothers with them
Like Drake said, "They past tense"
She's already had them

Tiempos como estos

Ella antes rezaba por tiempos como estos
Estar en paz y con sus zapatos bien puestos
Y con una sonrisa que se ve sin maquillaje
Ya no tiene que pretender
Porque se alejó de ellos que pretenden
Por fin dejo el pasado en el pasado
Que al cabo ya los callo
No hay necesidad encender una lumbre que ya no
alumbró

Fierce

I'm not doing what society wants me to do, so it fears
me
But I rather be feared than overlooked

Feroz

No estoy haciendo lo que la sociedad quiere que haga
Y les doy miedo, dicen que soy feroz
Y eso que todavía no han escuchado mi voz

A life without spice

Men once travelled across the world for me
Meanwhile, you let me go to waste as if there weren't plenty of others out there that wouldn't mind the smallest taste
Picture your life without spice... it's not that nice

Una vida sin sazón

Hombres cruzaron el mar en busca de mi sabor
No sabes cuantos quisieran tan siquiera un poquito de
mi sazón
Imagina tu vida sin sabor
Que dolor

Alone

I am not afraid of being alone
I pray alone, I think alone, I eat alone, I dream alone
See, I've been alone
I've let my tears dry in the sun
My worries wash away in the rain
And I wear my stress in my hair
My messy, curly, beautiful hair
But I'm not alone
I have never felt alone, because love has always been within me
It is just a matter for a beautiful soul to bring out what is already in me

Sola

Yo no tengo miedo de estar sola
Reso sola, pienso sola, como sola, y sueño sola
Pero nunca he estado sola
Porque el sol a secado mis lágrimas
Y la lluvia me a limpiado de preocupaciones
Y mi pelo esconde todos mis temores
Este pelo despeinado, chino, y sedoso, esconde todas mis imperfecciones
Yo nunca me he sentido sola, porque el amor vive dentro de mi
Solo hace falta que un alma hermosa me saque lo que ya vive en mi

Note to self

I'd rather let you go, than myself
I am more important

To anyone battling between their heart and their happiness.
Find you, lose them.

Nota personal

Prefiero dejarte ir que dejarme a mi
Yo importo mas

Si te encuentras en una batalla con tu corazón y tu felicidad.
Es mejor dejar a esas malas vibras que perderte tu misma.

2 THE GOOD/ LO BUENO

Wet dreams

If you've woken up with my name on your lips
It's just your heart telling you that it has never had love like this
So go back to sleep my love, and take this

Ensueños

Si algún día te has despertado de tus sueños
Solo es tu corazón diciéndote que soy la mujer de tus
sueños

Bounced checks

Waste my time and I will write you off like a check
I like consistency like my paychecks
I don't have time for bounced checks

Cheques devueltos

Yo no tenia tiempo para los juegos
Por eso lo tire como un cheque devuelto
Porque a mi me gustan los hombres constantes tanto como
me gustan mis cheques de pago, bien pagados
Esos nunca se van de mi lado

Not interested

She's just not that into you
If she was interested, she would never leave your messages
on read
She would remember everything that you said
She would send you random pictures just because
She'll have you thinking she's falling in love
But she's not that into you
Don't read between the lines
Because 10 times out of 9
She's just being nice…

No esta interesada

Ella no esta interesada
Porque si lo estaba
Te contestara todas tus llamadas
Y todo lo que le decías, nunca se le olvidaría
Pero no esta interesada
Ya cuelga esa llamada…

Don't come for me

What makes your heart melt
What makes your soul light up when it's felt
I'm so tired of shallow and superficial
Give me that charm, that charisma
If you don't have it, I'll show you where to get some
I'm too old fashioned for this
If you're coming for me, just know I'm not with this new
ish

No vengas por mí

Si no me puedes decir de las cosas que hacen tu corazón derretir
Y tu alma sonreír
No vengas por mi
Porque no tengo tiempo para hablar de cosas sin sentido
Solo de cosas bonitas que se pueden decir en el oído

I will learn

Lie to me
I'll figure it out soon
Forget me in the am
I'll recover by noon
Leave without saying goodbye
I'll learn how to not give a damn about you instead of cry
Take me for granted
I'll differentiate what a real man is
Hurt me
And I promise that will be the last day I'll let you have this

Aprenderé

Miénteme, que al cabo me doy cuenta
Olvidame por tu negligencia
Y me la pagaras sin que te des cuenta
Si te vas sin despedirte de mi
Te prometo que nunca te vuelvo a dar el regalo de verme
sonreír
Cuidado porque si me lastimas, me va valer todo madre
Y ya no volveré a consentirte, que te complazca tu madre

Irreplaceable

Don't lose me entertaining others
Unless you want to spend the rest of your life finding my replacement
So before you make that mistake, ask yourself if you got that kind of patience

Insustituible

No me pierdas por andar entreteniendo a otras
Si me llegas a perder, te vas a pasar el resto de tu vida
buscando a alguien como yo para reemplazarme
Pero antes de ser una estupidez, pregúntate si tienes ese
tipo de paciencia

His rib

Most men will lose their rib looking for thighs and breasts
If all he wanted is a 2 piece, well Popeyes is just around the
way
God makes no mistakes
Why risk losing a woman that gives, but never takes

Su costilla

Muchos hombres pierden su costilla por andar en busca de
pechos y piernas
Pero para que perder a una mujer que te da todo y nunca se
queja
No pierdas a tu costilla por una pierna
Porque al rato vas a andar de rodillas
Y ella con la cabeza tan alta que ya ni te mira

Pay attention

You may forget everything I ever said, but you will never, ever forget the way I made you feel
It was real wasn't it?
I know you still feel it

Pon atención

Quizás te olvidaras te todo lo que dije
Pero nunca vas a olvidar como te hice sentir
Y como te sentiste
Verdad que ahora te das cuenta que si me quisiste?

No regrets

I never feel regret when it's time to walk away
I know I tried
I gave it a thousand tries
But you gave me a million whys

No me arrepiento

Yo nunca me siento arrepentida cuando me voy
Yo sé que trate
Trate miles de veces
Pero tu me diste un millón de razones

Goals

A man that will break a thousand hearts just to keep mine
whole
Not caught up in my physical but my beautiful soul
Now that's goals

Metas

Un hombre que pueda romper miles de corazones, solo
para sostener el mío entero
Un hombre que no está entretenido con mi cuerpo pero
más con mi alma
Esas si son metas

Blame me

I know I am different
I am water you never swam in before
You're not accustomed to this love, no… not the way I do
it
You've never had something this real, so I guess I can't
blame you for not knowing what to do with it

Echame la culpa

Yo se que soy diferente
Tu nunca has navegado por estos lados
Se que no estas acostumbrado
Tu corazón nunca ha alumbrado
Por eso ni te puedo culpar por no saber como comportarte
Echame la culpa, pero déjeme amarte

Let's talk, not argue

I will never love a man enough to argue with him
He better watch his tone or find himself alone
You raise your voice at me, I'll raise my standards on you

Hablemos, no discutamos

Yo nunca voy a amar un hombre tanto como para discutir
Baja la vos si no quieres verme ir
Porque si me levantas la voz, yo levanto mis normas

I like you

I made myself accessible to you
Because I like your energy
I granted you access into my world
So don't lose your privilege

Me gustas

Me hice accesible para ti
Porque me gusto tu energía
Solo acuerdate que te di acceso
Pero si te portas mal, te quito este privilegió

Mr. Right

Sometimes, I question if I said no to Mr. Right
But then I think to myself, one of us should have
known… right?

El hombre para mí

Quizás le dije que no al hombre para mi
Pero me pongo a pensar, ¿Qué, no lo sabrá?
Porque nunca me busco
Entonces el hombre para mí, todavía no lo conozco

What comes around goes around

Not everything that looks good is good for you
Like water; if you drink too much of it you'll drown
But never overlook a good woman, they don't ever come
back around

Lo que viene va dando vueltas

No todo que parece bien es bueno para ti
Estarás bueno pero no para mi
Si tomas mucha agua te puedes ahogar
Pero nunca dejes una buena mujer pasar
Esas ya no vuelven… jamás

For the better

Sometimes, it takes a minute to understand that you
deserve better
First you will fight it, but then watch how things will
change for the better

Para lo mejor

A veces la única conclusión que necesitas después de terminar una relación es entender que mereces mejor
Primero va doler, pero después te va cambiar para lo mejor

No love lost

I no longer feel sad when I lose someone that didn't love
me
Instead, I feel bad they lost someone that loved them
Because they are about to find out how hard it is to find
this

Amor no perdido

Ya no me da lastima cuando pierdo a alguien que no me
amó
Ahora me da lastima que ellos perdieron a alguien que si los
quizo
Porque se van a dar cuenta lo difícil que es encontrar esto

Give up

You can try your hardest to get your message across,
But sometimes they just won't get it
So when your efforts become unmatched,
And your heart no longer seems to want it or react,
It's ok to give up
It's ok to no longer give a... middle finger up

Rendirse

No hay nada malo con rendirse
Cuando tus esfuerzos no son igualados
Y tu alma se siente como si se haya ido de tu lado
Esta bien rendirse
Esta bien que te valga madre y de reírte

Not at all

Even though she cannot erase him from her memory
she got rid of it all
The messages, the photos
Why hold onto someone that's never held onto her at
all?

De ningún modo

Aunque no pueda borrarlo de su memoria, borro todos
los mensajes y fotos
Para que aferrarse a un hombre que nunca te tuvo en su
mente menos en su corazón
Mejor tira todo a la basura y los recuerdos borralos

Game over

I used to lose sleep over you
I used to cry every morning that I didn't wake up next to
you
Until one day, I did it to you
You never looked at me the same, did you?
But now you know that it hurt me, and you can hurt, too

Se acabo el juego

Antes no podía dormir por tu culpa
Amanecía llorando, pensando "¿Donde estas?"
Hasta que un día, te lo hice a ti
Nunca me miraste igual
Pero ahora sabes que duele
Porque te la pasaste pensando… "¿Con quien duerme?"

The best

I would be lying if I said I wish you the best
But I do wish you lessons learned
See, you didn't deserve the best
Otherwise, I wouldn't have left

Lo mejor

Estuviera mintiendo si dijera que te deseo lo mejor
Pero si te deseo lecciones aprendidas
Es que tu no mereces lo mejor
De lo contrario, no me hubiera ido

3 THE BAD/ LO MALO

Closed mouths don't get fed

They say no response is a response
But just hit me with it, good or bad, I'll respond
I just want to feed you love
But if you keep leaving words unsaid
How will I ever know if you've been fed?

Bocas cerradas no se alimentan

Dicen que aunque no te den una respuesta, el silencio es una respuesta
Pero mejor dame una respuesta
Aunque sea mala o buena
Porque yo solo quiero alimentarte con amor
Pero si dejas palabras sin decir, ¿Como voy a saber si esta lleno tu corazón?

Misunderstood

We were never taught to understand each other
Because while a woman was taught to love and nurture,
A man was taught to be tough and not show emotion;
you know, for the culture
A woman was taught to be soft and to attend
A man hardly ever knows what words to say or how to
make amends
Relationships could all be so simple
If both would just put their pride aside and watch how
listening and understanding, suddenly becomes less
difficult…

I was taught to love you, you were taught to protect
Yet it's the same heart that you were suppose to protect
that you continue to neglect

Mal entendidos

Nunca nos enseñaron como entendernos
La mujer sabe amar y ser cariñosa
Porque desde niñas nos enseñan como ser una buena esposa
Mientras a los hombres les enseñan como ser fuerte
Pero no fuerte de la mente
¿Será por eso que no nos entendemos?
¿Será la razón que cuando nos peleamos nos hacemos de menos?
Todo sería más fácil si ponemos el orgullo a un lado…

A mi me enseñaron como amar y a ti como proteger
Pero es mi corazón que debes de proteger que no sabes ni como entender

Quiet lips

My heart no longer skips a beat when it sees you, but my body shivers
I'll never forget the day your energy told me what your lips couldn't quiver
You've never held back from bursting anyone's bubble
So when your lips silenced, I knew we were in trouble
You've never lied to me, so I will give you credit for remaining loyal at that
But it was your energy that couldn't lie, and I had no choice but to face the facts

Tu energía no miente

Mi corazón ya no salta un latido cuando te ve
Mi cuerpo ya no tiembla cuando lo quieres ver
Nunca voy a olvidar el día que tu energía me dijo lo que
tus labios no pudieron decir
Nunca has tenido pelos en la boca pero esta vez ni
podías mentir
Sabia que estábamos en peligro
Quizás ya te enfadaste de lo mismo… como yo

Consensual

Love is nice
But before I ever love a man again, I'll think twice
My love stories have been nothing but a series of
unfortunate events
So the next time I give a man my love, I will ask for
consent
How could someone not want this good loving, it just
doesn't make sense
But the issue wasn't accepting my love, it was reciprocation
I've had men accept my love like it was some donation
This isn't charity
Love like mine is a rarity
If I give it to a man, then it's not for free
So reciprocate, or let go of me

Igualmente

El amor es bonito
Pero antes de volver a amar otra vez voy a pensar un poquito
Mis historias de amor han sido nada mas que eventos de tragedias
Como puede ser que alguien no me quiera
Pero aceptar mi amor no es el problema
Es que no recibo amor, como que me la paso no mas en una lista de espera
Esperando un donador que nunca va venir
Será porque todo quieren gratis
Pues ni modo, porque no soy fácil
Pero ya se que para la otra, si no recibo el amor que doy igualmente,
Pues lo mando mucho a la chingada, que al cabo, tanta pinche gente

It's your heart

How about you just treat her heart as if it were your own
I bet you would be more careful

Es tu corazón

Porque no te imaginas que su corazón es tu corazón
Te apuesto que lo cuidaras mucho mejor

Signs

Last night I dreamt that a man I know proposed to me
Maybe it's time I let that go
Maybe it's my soul trying to tell me something I don't
know

Listen to your dreams

Sígnos

Anoche soñé que un hombre que conozco me pidió
matrimonio
A lo mejor es tiempo de dejar eso en paz
A lo mejor es mi alma tratando de decirme algo que nunca
me he imaginado… jamás

Escucha tus sueños

Man in the mirror

If you're always blaming someone else, then your mirror must be dirty… clean it

El hombre en el espejo

Si siempre andas echándole la culpa a otra persona, quizás tu espejo esta sucio… limpialo

Airplane Mode

You've been catching flights expecting her to stand by
As if she was going to wait for you until the end of time

Commit already, or let her go

Modo Avión

Tu has tomado vuelos pensando que ella te va esperar
La amas cuando estas pero te olvidas de ella cuando te
vas
Crees que va estar cuando regreses…
Pero no te va estar esperando para siempre
Así es que, comprometete o déjela en paz

Mind games

Holding back emotions to keep from getting hurt
I should have asked if you wanted my love first
Now it hurts, and it's changing me
My heart was never built for these games of hide and seek

Juegos mentales

Conteniendo mis emociones para no lastimarme
Te haya preguntado primero si querías mi amor desde un
principio
Pero ahora me duele porque mi corazón nunca estaba
listo para estos juegos mentales
Nunca he podido esconder emociones que no son de
juego, sino reales

In your feelings

He won't always be charming
You won't always look your best
Good sex will not fix everything
But the greatest relationships lasted because they put in the
work
Emotions come and go,
But it's not love that hurts
It is the people and their feelings that do

Tus emociones

El no siempre va ser simpático
Y tu no siempre vas hacer encantadora
Las mejores relaciones duraron porque los dos pusieron
el esfuerzo
Emociones van y vienen
Pero el amor no es lo que duele
Son las personas y sus emociones

Loyalty

Unless your loyalty got them treating you like royalty
Never let your loyalty keep you prisoner
Never give someone that much respect and love while they're too busy sharing it with him or her

Lealtad

No te hagas prisionero por tu propia lealtad a una persona
Para que darle tanto respeto y amor a alguien que lo
comparte con otras
Que te trate como realeza
O déjelo como un perro, y que le de otra de tragar

In another life

Maybe in another life, my love is reciprocated
Maybe in another life, I will never be kept waiting
Maybe in another life, I will not be taken for granted
Maybe in another life they won't just walk away, but rather step up and handle it

En otra vida

Quizás en otra vida mi amor será correspondido
Quizás en otra vida mi amor será anunciado a los 4
vientos y no al escondido
Quizás en otra vida no me van hacer de menos
Quizás en otra vida me quedaran deberes y no de mentís
o de lejos

Earn your presence

I no longer have time to entertain loose ends
I no longer have the energy to play house for pretend
I no longer have patience for silly mind games
I no longer hold onto hope, so leave just how you came
I'm not charging you rent, but to stay here you have to earn your presence…
Unless you don't want these presents

Gana tu presencia

Ya no tengo tiempo para estar entreteniendo a cabos
sueltos
Ya no tengo tiempo para estar jugando casita con mensos
Ya no tengo paciencia para los juegos
Ya no tengo esperanzas de ti, así es que así como vienes te
me vas
No te cobre renta, pero para hastar aquí conmigo tienes
que ganar tu presencia

I bet you think of me now

I remember all the times you ignored my calls and left me
at night all alone
I bet now you only wish my name would appear across the
screen of your phone

Ahora sí piensas en mí

Me acuerdo de todas las veces que ignoraste mis llamadas
Y todas las noches que me dejabas sola, y tu con otra como
si nada
Te apuesto que ahora le pides a la virgen que mi nombre
aparezca en la pantalla de tu teléfono
Estoy segura que hasta me lloras… Tengo razón… ¿si o
no?

The artist

Once I met a man that made me feel so sexy
I felt passion through my veins whenever he was next to
me
The way he looked at me and touched
It was like that feeling you get when you're drinking, but
not too much
Love or lust, I don't know, but…
He enjoyed leaving my clothes at my ankles
As he admired all my angles
I liked the view from the top
He was the artist, I was his workshop

El artista

Conocí un hombre que me hacia sentir tan atractiva
Lo extrañaba cada vez que me iba
El modo en que me miraba
La pasión que sentía cuando me tocaba
Un sentimiento como si estuviera tomada, pero no tanto
El le encantaba dejar mi ropa a mis tobillos y escuchar
mi llanto
A mi me gustaba la vista desde arriba
Yo era el lienzo y el el artista

Stalker

There is a fine line between a consistent man and a stalker
A stalker will not wish me the best unless I am his
A stalker does not really want to see me happy, unless it's
him who has me
That's not love; it is an obsession
It's their own state of mind that one should question
Know the difference between a consistent man and one
that just doesn't understand

*Do not put anything past these types of people; they're lost and pure
evil*

Acosador

Hay una diferencia entre una persona consistente y un
acosador
Un acosador solo me desea lo mejor y quiere verme feliz,
pero solo si estoy con el
Un acosador pretende
Un acosador le faltan tornillos en la mente
Eso no es un hombre consistente, eso es obsesión, eso es
un acosador

Cuidado con estos tipos, están perdidos y son pura maldad

Too emotional

Quit being so emotional
So emotional that you don't even know what you're feeling
Too emotional that you rather run away instead of face the
feelings
Too afraid of your own feelings
Too hesitant to show your true feelings
Baby, who hurt you? Who got you defensive?
My heart is open and it's made a home for you, so come in
Quit being so emotional
Quit walking away from someone that loves you
and wants you to have and to hold
Baby, just come home

Demasiado sentimental

Deja de ser tan sentimental
Tan sentimental que ni sabes lo que estas sintiendo
Eres tan sentimental que prefieres correr en ves de
enfrentar esas emociones
Pero para todo hay razones
Amor, quien te lastimo, porque siempre estas a la defensa?
Mi corazón esta abierto e hizo un hogar para ti, ven…
regresa
Deja de ser tan sentimental
Deja de huir de alguien que te ama, y regresa a casa

Hide and seek

You don't pay people off if you're innocent
You dont apologize to only do it again
You don't prey on the weak
Eventually what you keep trying to hide, the brave will seek
What is done in the dark will one day come to light,
Because even the devil cannot disguise himself in broad daylight

Al escondido

Un inocente no paga a las personas para callarlos
Un arrepentido no pide disculpas solo para volverlo
hacer
Tampoco ataca a los débiles una y otra vez
Lo que tu escondes, los valientes lo van a buscar
Y lo que haces en lo oscuro saldrá algún día a la luz
Porque ni el diablo puede disfrazerse en plena luz

Half of me

It's time I let go of what isn't for me
To take things as they are and not for what they seem
For a long time I've held onto what could be,
But now I understand that this is how it's gonna be
It's time I let go and take back all of me
You were gifted the best part of me,
Yet you only wanted parts of me
I've feared of losing you, when you never feared of losing
me
Maybe it's because you think you have me
Maybe it's because you think they're just going to pass up
on me
Until you get tired of going through women that aren't
even half of me

La mitad de mi

Es tiempo de dejar lo que no es para mi
De tomar todo como lo es y no como parece
Ya no me voy a detener
Por mucho tiempo me detuve a lo que podíamos ser
Pero ahora entiendo que esto es lo que es
Es tiempo de recuperar todo de mi
Te regale la mejor parte de mi
Pero tu solo querías partes de mi
Tuve miedo de perderte, cuando mi nombre ni pasaba por
tu mente
Será porque piensas que me tienes
Será porque piensas que todos los demás van y vienen
Será porque piensas que siempre voy a estar aquí
Hasta que tu te cansas de meterte con mujeres que ni son la
mitad de mi

I'll give up when you do

They say you're not supposed to give up on someone you
love
But if you ever feel like leaving me, I will be the one
holding the door open for you
Did you think I was going to beg for you to stay?
No, I'm good, but move out of the way
The next one is on his way

Yo me rendiré cuando tu lo hagas

Dicen que no debes de renunciar a alguien que amas
Que por lo bueno y lo malo y echarle ganas
Pero si algún dia me quieres dejar, yo te sostengo la puerta
Porque de rogarte, ni muerta
Que pensabas que te iba rogar, pues estas equivocado
Porque ya viene el otro, así es que échate para un lado

Acceptance

Never fall in love with potential
Too many times I obsessed about what someone could
be, but they won't be, and don't want to be
You can't change someone
Accept it, accept them, or move on

Aceptar

Nunca te enamores con la potencial de alguien
Muchas veces estuve obsesionada con lo que podía ser
Pero no puedes cambiar a nadie
Aceptalo, aceptalos, o sigue adelante

The other woman

The thrill of wanting someone that belongs to someone else
Be careful what you wish for
Is this how you want your daughter to carry herself?

La otra

La emoción de querer a alguien que pertenece a otra
persona
Ten cuidado con lo que deseas
Porque muchas veces no sabes lo que en realidad te espera
Es así como quieres que se lleve tu hija…
Cuidado mija

Trophies

Proud you are of those trophies
But if you were stripped of all your plaques and trophies
Who would you be?
If they took it all away
Would you still be the man you were yesterday, today?

Trofeos

Eres muy orgulloso de tus placas y trofeos
Pero quien serías si te quitaran todas tus placas y trofeos
¿Serias el mismo hombre,
O algo escondes?

Unclaimed Property

She thought she was special to him
But it was all in her mental, and not his
The feeling of knowing you're worth gold
But the man you're giving your all to is too busy being
entertained by knock offs and fake gold

Let him go, for one day he will find out the true weight
of gold

Propiedad no reclamada

Ella pensaba que era especial
Pero solo lo era en su mente
Ese sentimiento de saber que vales oro
Pero el hombre al quien le estas dando todo
Esta muy entretenido con plata chafa y no de oro

Dejalo, que alcabo algún día se va dar cuenta lo que pesa
el oro

4 THE BEAUTIFUL/ LO HERMOSO

Most men

"He's no good for you...
What he did to her he will do to you...
He will never change..."
I've heard it all, but I've chosen to learn the hard way
See, I do believe that men can change
I've seen an alcoholic stumble in his lies
To now walk by faith, and pray to the Most High
I know of a notorious womanizer
Who settled down with a woman he now loves and admires
I'll never hold the past against any man
Regardless of how many women he's ran
Sometimes, it takes the stars to align
But sometimes, most men just need time

To the first man that ever broke my heart, my father.
I am so proud of the man you have become.

Algunos hombres

"El no es bueno para ti…
Te va ser mas llorar que sonreir…
El nunca va a cambiar…"
Y te va poner los cuernos cuando no mires y cuando no
estas
Pero yo no hago caso a lo que me dice la gente
Porque yo si creo que hombres pueden cambiar de actitud
y de mente
Yo conocí un hombre que fue un alcohólico y luego dejo la
pisteada
Y un mujeriego que ya dejo de los juegos y esta con una
mujer que adora y ama
Yo nunca voy a juzgar a un hombre por su pasado
Y ni me importa cuantas mujeres ha tenido a su lado
Muchos hombres de niños nunca han tenido buen
ejemplos
Y por eso algunos hombres solo necesitan mas tiempo

*Para el primer hombre que rompió mi corazón, mi papá. Estoy tan
orgullosa del hombre que eres hoy.*

Beautiful soul

I gave into you every time
Without question, I will give you a thousand tries
I would love you until I'm worn down to my soles
Because to me, your flaws were nothing compared to your beautiful soul
I hope the woman you choose to share your life with can overcome your flaws,
For they are like unforeseen obstacles
If she is weak, loving you will seem impossible
And she will fall
I hope she never hurts you, as you can easily be misunderstood
I hope she can see you in this light, the way that I could
For it was through your eyes that I could see your heart
It has always been in the right place, but like an engine with no power
It needed me to start

Alma hermosa

Me entregue a ti cada vez
Te daría oportunidades, mas de tres
Te amaré hasta que se me acaben las suelas de mis zapatos
Porque para mí, tus imperfecciones no eran nada
comparado a tu alma hermosa
No es cualquier cosa
Ojala que la mujer a quien se lo entregues pueda ver mas de
tus imperfecciones
Y que tenga paciencia para aprender de tus buenas
intenciones
Porque es fácil de mal interpretarte
Y si no es fuerte, se l va ser mas difícil amarte
Pero yo vi tu corazón por tus ojos
Siempre ha estado en su lugar, pero como un motor sin
potencia
Necesitaba una mujer como yo, con paciencia

Friendship over love

Just tell me you love me to my face
Let my smile be the birth place
Hearing it just does something different
Your actions sometimes tell me, but words make a
difference
See, I don't want to fall in love with you if you're not
willing to try,
Because I will choose our friendship over love, just to not
ever have to say goodbye
I don't ever want to say that to you
But what I do want to say is "I love you"
And I would love to call you mine,
But if you don't see me in that light, then I will be your
friend until the end of time

Amistad sobre amor

Dime que me quieres en mi cara
Que mi sonrisa sea la razón en porque me amas
Escuchándolo a veces se siente diferente
Tus acciones me lo dicen, pero quiero escuchar tus
palabras; quiero quitarme esta inquietud de mi mente
Porque yo no me quiero enamorar de ti si no lo quieres
tratar
Prefiero nuestra amistad sobre amor
Prefiero nunca tener que decir adiós
Porque lo que te quiero decir es que te amo, y que quiero
que seas todo mío
Pero si no me vez en la misma luz, de todos modos seguiré
queriéndote, pero como amigos

Hold us accountable

Even when I am angry
I still want him next to me
Because I know we will get through it
It's just a matter of holding each other to it

Hacernos responsables

Aunque este molesta con el
Todavía lo quiero junto a mi
Porque se que esto va pasar y vamos estar bien
Solo es cosa de hacernos responsables

Be his peace

Beautiful black man
Eyes of chocolate, palms of sand
Let me be your peace
For you will never feel the need to fight with me
I will never discriminate or disappoint you, or anger you
like the ignorant people of this world do
I will not judge you, or make you feel insecure or unworthy
Because when you hurt, it hurts me
I know the world can be ugly, so when you can no longer
stand from constantly getting beat down,
or when you can no longer see,
I will hold you up, and like God, part the sea
For I will be your peace
There will be no need to ever fight with me

Seré su paz

Hombre hermoso de color
Ojos como el café, manos quemadas del sol
Déjame ser tu paz
Porque conmigo nunca tendrás que pelear, jamás
Yo no te voy a discriminar o decepcionar, como la gente
ignorante de este mundo
Yo no te voy a juzgar o serte sentir inseguro, o indigno
Porque a mi también me duele verte herido
Yo se que este mundo puede ser injusto
Pero si algún día ya no puedes seguir o ver, yo te levantare
y como Dios, apartaré el mar
Porque yo seré tu paz
Nunca tendrás que pelear conmigo, jamás

Forever you

You've seen me with no makeup on and you still think I'm cute
You've seen my attitude and you still haven't given me the boot
But now that you've seen all my flaws, will you love me anyway?
Will you hold me when the clouds are grey?
Will you remind me that I am strong, but even if I fall, it's ok?
Because you are here to stay
Will you hold the doors open for me for years to come?
Will you hold my hand in public like we're still sprung?
Will you commit to never introducing me to anything you can not keep up with?
Will you promise to stay forever the man that I fell in love with?

Siempre tu

Tu me has visto sin maquillaje, y aun así piensas que estoy
bonita
Tu has visto mi actitud, y aun asi no me has mandado a la
jodida
¿Pero me vas a seguir queriendo ahora que ya vistes todas
mis imperfecciones?
¿Me vas a seguir amando cuando no entiendo razones?
¿Me vas a seguir abrazando cuando las nubes estén color
gris y cuando me haga falta sonreír?
¿Me vas a seguir recordando que soy fuerte pero si me
caigo es ok?
Porque tu vas a estar allí
¿Me vas a seguir abriendo las puertas y tomándome de la
mano cuando salgamos?
¿Podrás cometer a nunca introducirme a cosas que no vas a
poder seguir haciendo?
Prometeme que vas hacer el mismo hombre con el que yo
me enamore
Prometeme que vas a ser siempre tu, una y otra vez

Heart Overseas

Your scent lingers wherever I rest my head
At night I find myself on your side of the bed
Throughout my day I envision your smile
Knowing that I won't get to see it again for a while
I try not to think of the time that has to pass,
Which is why when you're here, I overwhelm you with love like it's my last
It's hard when you're away
I long for the day that you come back, but not to visit
To stay

Corazón en el extranjero

Tu aroma perdura donde quiera que descanso mi cabeza
Y en la noche me encuentro a en tu lado de la cama
y sudada como las noches esas
Durante mi día me imagino esa sonrisa
Sabiendo que no la voy a ver, y que tiene que pasar todo
este tiempo, sin prisa
Por eso cuando estas aquí te doy todo mi amor como si
se me fuera acabar
Es dificil cuando no estas
Espero tu regreso, pero no para que vengas de visita
Para que te quedes conmigo por siempre, mi vida

Be Her Peace

The highlight of her day
The sun when the skies are grey
Her moon and stars when it gets late
And the glow of her skin when she wakes
Be the peace her soul needs
as she places her trust in your eyes,
And release her love from within her thighs
Be her peace, her protector
Because like a flower in the winter,
it dies if you neglect her
Be her peace

Sea su paz

Sea el punto culminante de su día
Sea su sol cuando el cielo esta gris y cuando se sienta
agotada
Sea su luna y estrellas en la noche
Y el brillo de su piel cuando amanece
Sea la paz que ella necesita cuando te esta mirando a los
ojos
Y cuando liberas su amor de sus piernas
Sea su paz, su guardián
Porque como una flor en el invierno, se muere si la
descuidas
Sea su paz

To infinity and Beyond

No distance is too far
No time is too long
When you have 2 beautiful souls that cannot distinguish the
difference between when you're there to when you're gone
Your love should not change from when you're near to
when you're far
When you know what you have, obstacles just don't exist
So love me hard, and send me a kiss
I'll go to infinity, if you push us beyond this

Al infinito y mas allá

No hay distancia demasiado lejos
Ningun tiempo es demasiado largo
Cuando tienes a 2 almas hermosas que no pueden
distinguir la diferencia en cuando estas y cuando no lo estas
Tu amor no debería cambiar porque estas aquí o allá
Obstáculos no existen cuando sabes lo que tienes
Entonces te pido que me ames fuerte y mandame un beso
Porque yo iré al infinito si nos llevas mas allá de esto

I'd rather

It's hard for me to say I love you
when I'd rather show you
I'd rather hold you and murder you with kisses
I'd rather cook you your favorite meal
I'd rather show you with every smile and every stare
I'm usually selfish with my love, but with you I will share

Prefiero

Es difícil decirte que te amo cuando prefiero demostrartelo
Prefiero abrazarte y matarte con besos
Prefiero cocinar tu plato favorito
Y con cada mirada y sonrisa, te lo demuestro
Normalmente no le doy mi amor a nadie, pero contigo lo comparto
Así es como te demuestro, lo tanto que te amo

Unconditional

Love, without putting the burden of your past on their
shoulders
Love, like you have done over and over
Love, like you've never had your heart broken
Love, without comparison to your last
This is your future now, not your past
Love, without expectations for Valentine's Day,
For love is no holiday
There are no breaks or time restraints
So love, and don't be afraid
Put all your passion into it like it's the last piece of art
you will ever make
Love without restrictions, and love without conditions

Incondicional

Ama, sin poner la carga de tu pasado sobre sus hombros
Ama, como si lo has hecho una y otra vez
Ama, como si nunca te han roto tu corazón
Ama, sin compararlo con aquel cabron
Ama, sin expectativas para el día de San Valentin,
El amor no es un dia feriado
No hay descansos, o restricciones de tiempo
Así que ama y no tengas miedo
Ama con toda tu pasíon
Porque el amor no viene con restricciones o condiciones
Entonces ama y mejor deje que te enamoren

Honey

I just want to be the reason your smile never leaves your
face
How's that taste?
It's sweet, huh…

Miel

Yo solo quiero ser la razón en que tu sonrisa nunca deja
tu rostro
Como te sabe eso?
Mieloso…

Love you anyway

It's easy to find somebody these days
It doesn't take much but a swipe to the right
But try finding somebody that will stick around
long enough to notice all of your flaws and see if
they will stay and love you anyway

De todos modos

Es fácil encontrar a alguien hoy en día
Solo desliza a la derecha
Pero ve y busca alguien que se quede a verte en tus fachas y
toda fea
A ver si en verdad te quiere o si se va con ella

Your efforts

The most attractive thing to me is effort
The effort to get to know me
The effort to see me
The effort to open up your soul to love me
Put in the effort, and I'll put in the time

Sus esfuerzos

Lo mas atractivo para mi son sus esfuerzos
El esfuerzo por conocerme
El esfuerzo por venir a verme
El esfuerzo de abrir tu alma para amarme
Si tu pones el esfuerzo
Yo pongo el tiempo

Lead me

Lord knows I want my son to have your eyes
Beautiful brown eyes
Lord knows I want my son to have your complexion
Beautiful melanin
Lord knows I seek protection, and that's in your arms
Lord knows I seek for peace, and that's in your soul
Lord knows I seek for comfort, and that's on your chest
Lord knows I'm independent, but if you lead, I will follow
Because if God placed you before me, I promise to love you today, yesterday, and tomorrow

Guíame

Dios sabe que quiero que mi hijo tenga tus ojos
Ojos hermosos, color café
Dios sabe que quiero que mi hijo tenga el color de tu piel
Como azúcar morena con chocolate y miel
Dios sabe que busco protección, y eso esta en tus brazos
Dios sabe que busco paz, y eso esta en tu alma
Dios sabe que busco consuelo, y eso esta en tu pecho
Dios sabe que soy muy independiente, pero si tu me
guias, yo te sigo, y juntos vamos lejos
Porque si Dios fue el que te trajo a mi
Te prometo que te amaré hoy como ayer, como mañana
y hasta el fin

3 kisses

Those kisses before work kind of love
Those kisses when she comes home kind of love
Those kisses before you leave to chill with the boys
kind of love
Sometimes you don't have to say you love them, it just
shows

3 *besos*

Esos besos que te doy antes de irme al trabajo
Esos besos que nos damos cuando regresamos
Esos besos que me das antes de irte a salir con los
muchachos
No siempre nos tenemos que decir que nos queremos,
Si nuestro amor esta en cada beso

Lost and found

I've always been afraid of deep waters, until the day I looked into your eyes
Never in my life have I gone so deep and not been afraid to drown
Your eyes are like a lost and found;
Dark enough to get lost in,
But like city lights, bright enough to guide me through

Objetos perdidos

Siempre he tenido miedo de las aguas profundas
Hasta el día en que miré en tus ojos
Nunca en mi vida he ido tan profundo sin que me diera
miedo
Tus ojos son como objectos perdidos, pero no me he
pierdo
Oscuros como la noche, pero alumbrantes como luces
en la cuidad
No me perdí, porque allí estas

Chocolate

Chocolate brown eyes,
Won't you just stare into mine?
Let's pretend nothing else is around us,
Let's pretend the world revolves around us
I gave myself to you when I was already happy,
But you, my love, are my bonus

Chocolate

Ojos de chocolate
Mirame a los ojos
Hay que pretender que solo estamos nosotros
Supongamos que el mundo gira a nuestro alrededor
Me entregué a ti cuando ya era feliz
Pero tú, mi amor, eres mi bono

Just love me

Love me as much as I do
Love me like how I love you
Love me with no restrictions
Make love to me like an addiction
Love me like you'll lose me tomorrow
Love me as much as I did yesterday, and will tomorrow
Love me like I'm perfect
Love me because I'm worth it
Love me and don't hold back
I've never loved like this either, until I witnessed how your soul and mine react
Just love me

Solo ámame

Ámame tanto como yo
Ámame como te amo
Ámame sin restricciones
Haz me el amor como una adicción
Ámame como si fueras a perderme mañana
Ámame tanto como te ame ayer y te amare mañana
Ámame como si fuera perfecta
Ámame porque yo lo valgo
Ámame y no te contengas
Nunca he amado así tampoco, hasta que fui testigo de
como reaccionan tu alma y la mia
Solo ámame, vida mía

Souls

My soul yearns for yours when you're away
When you leave, it wants to scream "please stay"
I'm a movement by myself
But you are just so damn good for my health
I can never seem to get enough,
And I've never thought of giving up, not once
Time or distance doesn't seem to phase us
Everytime we meet, it's like we never left,
We just crave us
Your eyes make me feel so damn sexy
Your arms always remind me that you've never left me
And your smile blazes a fire deep in my soul
How could I ever let go?
I don't know what the future holds
All I know is that I need you to have and to hold

Almas

Mi alma anhela la tuya cuando no estás
Quiere gritar "no te vayas" cuando te vas
Es que eres tan bueno para mi salud
Mi medicina eres tu
El tiempo y la distancia no parecen ser una fase
Nos volvemos a enamorar cada vez que nos encontramos
Tanto tiempo que ha pasado, y aun todavía nos amamos
Tus ojos me hacen sentir tan bella
Tus brazos me recuerdan que de ese corazón, yo soy la
dueña
Y esa sonrisa que arde un fuego en lo profundo de mi alma
Yo no se lo que nos espera en el futuro
Solo se que mi corazón es tuyo

What you need

You need someone that will entangle all your secrets in her hair
You need someone that will show you love, that kind that says it with every stare
You need someone that can cook you your favorite meal
You need someone that makes her presence feel like home... that feel
You need someone that loves your soul hard enough to look past your flaws
You need someone that makes love to you so good you have to pause
You need someone that makes forever seem too short
You need someone that will travel to the end of the world with you – passport
You need someone that will keep you calm like herbal tea
Baby, what you need is me

Lo que necesitas

Tu necesitas a alguien que enrede todos tus secretos en su
cabello
Tu necesitas a alguien que te muestre amor no, importa si
estas cerca o lejos
Tu necesitas a alguien que te dará tu espacio y no te enfada
Tu necesitas a alguien que te dice te amo con cada mirada
Tu necesitas a alguien que te cocine tus platos favoritos
Tu necesitas a alguien que te vuelve loco tan siquiera un
poquito
Tu necesitas a alguien que te haga sentir siempre como en
casa
Tu necesitas a alguien que ame tu alma lo suficientemente
fuerte como para mirar más allá de tus defectos
Tu necesitas a alguien que contigo se va donde quiera, y
lejos
Tu necesitas a alguien que te tendrá calmado como el té de
yerba buena
Hombre carajo, que no ves que lo que tu necesitas soy yo,
la mas buena

Forever young

Catch me off guard
Like random Facetimes when I'm chilling with no makeup
on
And when you're wrong, make it right
But not with flowers or sorrys, don't be the mediocre type
More like sing me a love song that tells me how you feel
Sing it at the top of your lungs so I know it's real
Let's take late night drives with no destination
Let the moon be our spot light, for we are the show… the
sensation
Call the play, and I'll run it back
Let's be forever young, let's get that old thing back

Joven para siempre

Llámame cuando menos lo espero
Sin maquillaje y sin peinarme el pelo
Y cuando estés en el mal hazlo todo bien
Pero no con flores o disculpas, no seas mediocre
Mejor cantame una balada que me dice como te sientes
Vamos por allí en la noche sin rumbo
No importa si nos perdemos, porque estamos juntos
Hay que ser por siempre jóvenes
Seguir emocionados de amar como la primera vez

Love to love

I can't rush something that I want to last forever
Even God is taking his sweet time putting us together
I day dream of being loved the way I love
It's that kind of love many search for, but few get a hold
of
A passion that the average would drown in
A bond that most will lose, but we won't, because we
found it
I imagine one day being loved the way I love
But for that, you will have to love to love me
And that takes time, so for now just kiss and hug me

Amar al amor

Yo no puedo apresurar algo que quiero que dure para
siempre
Hasta Dios esta tomando su tiempo
Yo sueño con ser amada como amo
Es ese tipo de amor que muchos buscan, pero pocos
consiguen
Una pasión que muchos se ahogarían
Me imagino que algún día seré amada como yo amo
Pero para eso, tu tienes que amar al amarme
Y eso toma tiempo, entonces por ahorita besa y abrazame

Mine

You light a fire in my soul that only you can put out
I am the candles to your birthday cake, baby blow me
out
Come and hold this,
do as you please with me like you own this
I get off knowing that you are mine
But no two words have ever sounded more beautiful
than hearing you say "she's mine"

Mía

Enciendes un fuego en mi alma que solo tu puedes apagar
Soy las velas de tu pastel amor, apagame
Venga aquí y agarrame
Haz lo que quieras como si fueras dueño
Nada me excita mas que saber que eres todo mío, mi sueño
Yo nunca he escuchado unas palabras mas bonitas
Que cuando te escuche decir "ella es mía"

Sweeter than me

I used to crave for something sweeter than me,
And then God placed you before me

Look at God…

Mas dulce que yo

Antes deseaba algo más dulce que yo
Y luego Dios te puso delante de mí

Mira a Dios...

Brown sugar, honey, and gold

Give me your filthy mind, I wanna Dora explore it
Show me some substance, I wanna see what I am up against
Let our smiles be our public display of affection
Let our love show out in every which way and direction
I love to love you
Nothing has ever gone better with me than you
You're like my melatonin I take before bed
My day is complete once I feel your lips on my forehead
Loving you will never get old
You're my brown sugar, my honey, my gold…

Azúcar moreno, miel, y oro

Dame tu mente sucia, quiero explorarla como Dora la
Exploradora
Demuestrame tu sustancia
Dejemos que la risa en público sea nuestra muestra pública
de afección
Quiero perderme en acción
Pero contigo
Porque nada va mejor que tu conmigo
Eres como la melatonina que me tomo antes de dormir
Mi día está completo una vez que siento tus labios en mi
frente
Nunca me cansare de amarte, porque para mi eres todo
Mi azúcar moreno, mi miel, mi oro…

If you've never experienced love, then you will never understand my native tongue.

To be continued...

*Si nunca has experimentado el amor,
entonces nunca entenderás mi lengua
nativa.*

Continuará...

ABOUT THE AUTHOR

Maribel Sandoval is a Latin American poet who has been writing since she was in grade school. It wasn't until 2018 that she decided to share her writing with the world. She created a personal Instagram profile that she uses to post her thoughts, often dealing with love and relationships. She has gained wide popularity for her positive messages, witty tongue, and bilingual writing, reaching International followers.

32176861R00109

Made in the USA
Lexington, KY
28 February 2019